THE DESCENT

The Descent

Poetry by

SOPHIE CABOT BLACK

With best wishes —

[signature]

6th of November, 2004

Graywolf Press
Saint Paul, Minnesota

Publication of this volume is made possible in part by a grant provided by the Minnesota State Arts Board, through an appropriation by the Minnesota State Legislature; a grant from the Wells Fargo Foundation Minnesota; and a grant from the National Endowment for the Arts, which believes that a great nation deserves great art. Significant support has also been provided by the Bush Foundation; Target, Marshall Field's and Mervyn's with support from the Target Foundation; the McKnight Foundation; and other generous contributions from foundations, corporations, and individuals. To these organizations and individuals we offer our heartfelt thanks.

A Jane Kenyon book, funded in part by the Estate of Jane Kenyon
to support the ongoing careers of women poets published by Graywolf Press.

Special funding for this title has been provided by the Jerome Foundation.

MINNESOTA
STATE ARTS BOARD

NATIONAL
ENDOWMENT
FOR THE ARTS

Published by GRAYWOLF PRESS
2402 University Avenue, Suite 203
Saint Paul, Minnesota 55114
All rights reserved.

www.graywolfpress.org

Published in the United States of America

ISBN 1-55597-406-6

2 4 6 8 9 7 5 3 1
First Graywolf Printing, 2004

Library of Congress Control Number: 2004104186

Cover design: Jeanne Lee

Cover art: Hugo Simberg, *The Wounded Angel*, 1903
Ateneum Art Museum, Helsinki, Finland
Central Art Archives/Hannu Aaltonen

ACKNOWLEDGMENTS

Grateful acknowledgment is made to the editors of the following publications in which some of these poems have appeared: *Agni, The Atlantic, Bloom, Boston Review, Colorado Review, Columbia Magazine, Denver Quarterly, Fence, Gulf Coast, Lyric, The New Republic, Paris Review, Partisan Review, Ploughshares, Poetry, Post Road, Seneca Review, Vallum,* and *The Yale Review.*

"Birthday" appeared in *Birthday Poems: A Celebration,* ed: Shinder, Thunder's Mouth, 2001.

"The Hunt" will appear in *Never Before: Poems about First Experiences,* ed: Bosselaar, Four Way Books, 2005.

"Where We Cross" was part of *Poets & Writers: The Arts Respond to 9/11.*

"The Last Minute" & "When on the Third Night" was also part of *The Legacy Project.*

"As She Goes" appeared in *Doggerel: Poems about Dogs,* ed: Ciuraru, Everyman's Library, 2003.

"As She Goes" also received the Poetry Society of America's 1996 Medwick Award.

Many thanks to Radcliffe's Bunting Institute and other givers of care during the writing of this book.

Special thanks to Timothy Donnelly and Lucie Brock-Broido.

Also my deep gratitude to Jeffrey Shotts and Jason Shinder.

And to Diane, abiding.

For
Fiona and Roane Isabel

and for
Lucy Grealy and Stanley Kunitz

CONTENTS

II

III

For unto whomsoever much is given,
of him shall be much required.

—LUKE 12:48

THE DESCENT

AND THEN

You went on with your story as if someone
Still listened; you got up and walked
Back and forth, pausing by the garden wall

To see what would happen. And the lovers
Worked so deep into the night they forgot
Who brought them; they continued until the light
Finally arrived, unappeasable, and this time

Without you. That was how it began, the many voices
Gathering, the language you thought you invented
Breaking into noise no longer understood,

Never noticing the tree where birds
Grew unafraid, where you let yourself stray, the sun
In your eyes, the dust: you, who no longer knew
Where to go, how far you'd already come.

I

THE MOUNTAIN

Three men gather. To honor another who has died,
To set a stone in his favorite meadow.
They walk into mountains until coming to a field
Where one man decides to sit awhile. Two men
Continue up the watershed, speaking
Of women and hay and how it has been too long
Since the rains, even the elk have come down.
When they get to the next clearing, the second man
Climbs into a tree and falls asleep. He is tired
And does not want to be with the other.
Into the cold evening the third man rises, and the owl waits
Until she can no longer. He holds his hands
Over a fire he has built in the treeless North.
He is thinking of the descent, all of it.

THE TOOTH

No longer simple, if ever was. The coyote lies at the edge
Of the lake. I meant this, I did not; the death I paid for

Has come: a bad job of it, her jaw blown off, her underside
Gone, legs strung up with bailing twine, the body dragged

And quickly buried under leaves. When you pray, when you
Try to pray, words do not correspond in this crowded light,

They become slippery, wrong, not what I meant at all.
My knees sink in the muck, gut-blood and fur

Thicker than imagined, and out of the red wilderness
Of bone and tongue, one lone tooth more clean and white

Than God ever could be. No longer the heart
To take what I came for: the tooth so oddly rising

Out of a midst where the living cling
For whatever they can build of her until there is no trace.

THE LAKE

Day and night, the lake dreams of sky.
A privacy as old as the mountains
And her up there, stuck among peaks. Her whole eye

Fastened on hawk, gatherings of cloud or stars,
So little trespass. An airplane once
Crossed her brow; she searched but could not find

A face. Having lived with such strict beauty
She comes to know the sun is nothing
But itself and the path it throws; the moon

A riddled stone. If only a hand
Would tremble along her cheek, would disturb. Even the elk
Pass by, drawn to the spill of creeks below—

How she cannot help abundance, even as it leaves her,
As it sings all the way down the mountain.

THE HUNT

To be in the way, belonging. To wait
Until paths cross. The aspen do not know,
Despite what you heard or imagined

Before dawn. The idea: to be still
As stone. To enter the stand and not move
Until she finds you, to be darkness

And then light breaking in. One of you
Will make a mistake. And what happens remains
In a tree others walk by on their way to water
Or desire or perhaps to die, and even if you leave

With the ringing still in your ears,
Even if she is no longer wanted,
She enters you like a forgotten road;
She makes a bed on your tongue and lies down.

LOST

I am still here between the sun
That rises and the one that sets. To remain
Or go on. Which means to talk,

To remember wind, words for what happened,
How I could no longer figure you
From trees. And a turning of weather so quiet

I grew ashamed. I should have stayed with the horse
Huddled under ledge, but to go back now
Means to come upon myself. To be lost

Is to keep arriving. And so a trail becomes
All trails, perhaps a way out. Which is to say already
I am moving toward voices, each bend of the road

Made worse by knowing what I tell them
Will be different than what I've told myself.

HORSE, AGAIN

Strict in the idea of knowing where you head
I walk a certain direction. What
To call this symmetry, for I too diminish

When you are not to be found. I learn
To be ruthless finding your brown eye
In the thick leaves, your tail no longer

Blending with aspen. To run up against the end
Of the box canyon; I have prayed for
Your surrender like a priest. And this time
I do not want to be about damage, or strategy

Or even debt: I do not want this to be why
You remember. Each standing with the wide open
At our backs. Nothing you can give that I won't
Someday get. I let go the rope; I sit down.

FOR THE TAKING

Soon from rock a flower comes, gesture
For which not one reason is given, which goes

Beyond each storm and breath, curious
Into the waiting of no particular save the hand

That tears in. But if whatever moves
Is moved by mistake, then all would be

Wrong, which is not possible, not the wind, not
The mountain, not the angle of light which tells

The stranger to begin again, as he carries
The flower to the last without asking.

AFTER THE STORM

Before, I did not believe
In lightning, its work, the mad climb up from ground
Desperate to marry what descends. The sudden need

For more than one path, the white hand spread,
The elaborate delta. Before the storm,
I did not understand; I thought revelation

Would come later, just when I *wasn't* looking—
The way lightning is a trick to see
You for a moment, to tease
And scatter so all I think of

Is you, how I might have seen one side
Of your face, an eye glistening, a cheek
Upturned in rain, and I try to remember
That moment, and then beyond.

COUGAR

In this narrow passage I must appear as large
As possible, arms uplifted into what might

Be thought of as God and the idea of how
To get past even this without being killed,

Taken away, for somewhere in the act of want
Is being wanted, and we move

Over the frozen ground in the presumption
One of us will suffer and only one of us will be

Exact enough, which is why I came alone,
Following a creek back up its last place

To see how far I could go, with the raven
Who will not end his circle, the wind as it

Turns through a gnarl of bristlecone. We were
Never meant to be this close and to survive.

MORE THAN ONCE

In this tree are no indications
Of the chosen. Only the shine and black
Where lightning struck, where I lean as if

Some answer has been given, and now my fingers
Move across the mark to learn the site
Where this will never happen again. And yet

This too is wrong; once started, the electric
Easily returns to the carved place. The wound
Wants more wound, until the vein that fire enters

Becomes what cannot hold, what is then destroyed,
Which looks again and again for more weather,
The random dust, the illumination of being

Used, and us trembling at the ruins,
At the remains of one who took on such light.

IN HIGH COUNTRY

It is easy to think you have done well,
Moving along in the beautiful. So much to praise
By the fire before sleep. Until a severed pine,

Absence. This is how you remember
Where you are: the marked tree, watershed
Understood by map, altitude traced

Ring by ring. While at your back the trail
Lapses, even as you keep the mountain
In sight. Branches close, flower after flower
Rise again to their places. In this country

Each step becomes an argument
For the last. Your horse will not climb
Until you do, and when it is time,
He will only head back by how he came.

EAGLE

The eye rotates toward any small disturbance,
Tear in the fabric from which to take up

The easily bewildered. He has stared long
Into what lives below, the distance,

And does not remember which came first, hunger
Or the memory of hunger. Deep in a tree

He waits until everywhere is the quickening,
And he rises, for only in rising

Can the steep and necessary
Begin. To bear down, made instrument

By the outline he makes, leaving nothing
To chance. To come upon what trembles, to be

Precise in the beak or to have gone wrong
That particular evening by design.

WATCHING FOR SNAKES

Better to keep behind, careful on some trail
Becoming the color of what I move among.
I follow the one before me, tree

By blazed tree. Just ahead, a muletail quivers,
My eyes on each strand, any sign of newly bent
Branch or sudden velocity. The stick may turn

To snake, a voice cry out, and the brothers
I have mostly loved can kill, without ever looking back.
They move along the ridge with nothing to say,
Their boots covered in red dust. There is much

The ground refuses; a traveler passes by,
Makes out what remains, perhaps enough to turn
Back down to the valley, the prairie, the road
To the city, the light which breaks and asks for more.

COUNTING THE DARKER BIRDS

After the one crow, it is no longer
In my hands. To keep from the next bird,
Any black stain; to get away from the river,

From sifting bone, claw, a few left stars
Of blood or scat filled with bark. The smallest grief
Makes a church of each place broken,

Or unfinished, like following an old road
To see where it ends. Leaning down
From my horse I realize I have lost track;
Many are the signs to walk by. After

The first crow, it is too late: already I am
Hurrying, the little hands of cottonwood
Leaves turn in one direction, consider
Rain, darkness piling up in the trees.

HOME

Down from the search, the long recitals of ridge
Which are about solitude: cloudburst, a lament of wind
To vigil through, to move first by reason

Then grow wild in the thin grass, over fossil
And nowhere to lie without some animal
To find me. Perhaps too much has happened to return,

Or no one will ask. Down from the higher country,
Leaving steep meadows behind, the shifts
Of snow making a way to the river,
How stone by stone the cairns come undone,

No longer legible. And in the last light
The forest I must cross
Becomes many houses, a mist
Rising from each tree like hearthsmoke.

RATTLESNAKE

I cannot help my end, my noisy tremble,
One last bit of business, or faithful
Answer to some old question. Wanting out

In a kingdom of sun; no matter
How much I ask, no rock in sight, no sight
But what I already know. Only the unlocking

Of jaw to receive whatever crosses
My way. Footsteps heard from a far-off
Place, a voice muttering, alone

And without caution. I shake with work to do,
To stay, to move on; my skin follows like a veil.
Mine is the bite of the wrong turn; I am promised

No easy death and undertake my path as if
I am to come back, next time one of them.

THE HARROWING

To enter the field without speaking
Of the bad years is to trust what is

Buried, or at least sleeps. All I bring to dirt
Will rise again through green, what survives

The first plough. Also: an uncertain fawn
Or rabbit taken up and broken by tines

Becomes part of the work, held in morning
Light, thrown to the dog. We mend most everything

Known, marks in a field where we maintain
Others were before, also turning earth

So that one after another we rely on meaning
Nothing, even for what is left behind. In this place, to stay

Only as long as it takes; how to enter
And allow for leaving without getting caught.

GUN

After all done and not done, the long
Wait until morning where shape by shape
Returns the room and a gray horizon

Of window ledge. He was tired of holding
The steel drawn across the body as if
At the end of some orchestral work,

Still in the mouth a sentence he wanted
To finish. And he could not find the way
Back, in his hands the weight, the click

Of metal and lock. To pull over and rest
By the river was always in his mind,
To watch the rifle float before it dropped,

Disappeared. To look into the face as it rises
Up from river bottom, becoming clear.

PULLING INTO MORNING

As if a river twisting back upon itself,
The foal arrived as the mare died. One breath ends
At the start of another; one more way

Into the world. The sun rose, the song
Of the rooster broke over the barn,
And I kept at my notebook with any odd detail

Of labor, of transition. I carefully wrote
Until it became an old horse, an awkward colt
And a bad night. She may or may not have known
What she was carrying. She may or may not

Have heard your hooves hit ground.
Even in the earnest light of your rising, you will never know
How you came to be. You lean into my arms
Until I no longer feel them. There is no rest.

THE STRAY

Watch, said he, for the one cow
Still up the mountain— in time she will lead you
To those hidden. She does not mean

To be noticed; instead considers herself as blank
As the rock she stands in front of. Go up to her
With outstretched hand, said he, examine what you can:

The direction of track or dung, the marks
Burned into her side (to keep a body faithful)
And call out the given names, even as it grows dark. Do this
Until you can say nothing more could be done

Or at least until you are last to come down, for below
Moves a rider, his lamp to one side (he must look away
To see) searching for stragglers, driving them toward
Barn doors, wide open and waiting for the saved.

WHEN IT WAS TIME

He did not carry the body up, he could not,
After all it was a horse and so instead
He asked the horse to carry him

As far as possible, while the animal believed
They were on some mission, like searching
For poachers up on the ridge, or other signs

Of trespass, and with great difficulty
Breathed, climbed and kept turning
To see what the man was doing;

The horse that believed something ordinary
Was about to happen and the man who believed
He was moving into what he must now do

But suddenly found himself unable,
Having come to the place
Of one time too many, the terrain worn down

By many years of this, this love of another
Who will move, carry, or even bend when and wherever the man wishes.
He propped the gun up against the tree

As he sat in the dirt and the dark came on,
And the horse who watched was becoming changed
And later would go away knowing nothing ever bound him

To the rock up there, where what the man would do
And what he would not do still unravels.

THE CLIMB

I will be done with mountains. Let
The subsequent come, the fallen stone.
Let blazes heal, let erosion. Having marked

Certain places, it becomes easier to rest
On the way back down. What name to leave
This flower (or keep nameless), what small rock

To bring back to where I will write you
Of how it was, getting whatever remained
Up to the site we thought highest. The mountain

Does not move; nothing I can say
Will move it. Beyond are only more mountains
Conspiring as if to break free. And I cannot hear

For the noise of breath; each finger uncurls
And one blue flower where trees refuse to live.

AFTERWORLD

Starlight goes on, resolute. Dawn
Breaks the ridge. What could not be found
Is now everywhere. The mare,

The ragged slope, birds. A man rises from sleep, wonders
How he is necessary. Not one cow
Is missing. The herd waits by river's edge,

Their flanks luminous with morning; a sullen line
Of coyote-track finishes at the water. Closed
Are the eyes of horses; between their lips the crowns
Of thistle. Ridge by ridge, day congregates

As valley by valley, each man tends the last
Of his fire. As a tree grows at the gate, hardens
Around wire, as birds, ancient with intention,
Return to sing upon their branches.

II

THE TREE

And when we woke it was like nothing
Ever dreamt before this: wrist, neck,
The hollow behind the knee, your hair

Filling my hands, all of it while we turned
And turned until we were unforgivable,
Adamant with bark, as if a wayward god had come

Upon us, bewitching breast to breast, fingers
Still tracing a vein, a thigh
No longer intent on destination

But in the keep of one limb resting on another, breath
Lingering in leaves, at the edge of a road
Where we were once lost, your hand faithful

In its nest, your mouth on my mouth
Caught, our feet tangled, looking for earth.

BEFORE YOU

I kneel down
To understand what happens. It begins
With the mouth, always

Searching toward
What takes shape; while the hand
Continues to stalk,

Small arrests are made.
Do not speak; let silence.
Light fails in this awkward place

And I am here as no one
Has ever been before;
The worst that I watch

Myself survive.
You would have me
Do this, you who are so far

From myself, who keep
Each road possible until nothing is left
To regret.

HAVING MUCH

I know the shape you take
When you are near; I try once again
To become what you do not have,

And study the body, how it continues
While many walk by with heads down
As if written everywhere are the words

No one will use and the matter of what hands
Do not do. It is possible to suffer
Having much. It is possible to regret

The beauty that keeps one from staying long
And without mercy. How I want you to break
What builds, the still life of everything

In its place, so accurate you cannot help
But lie down, weary of what you make me.

BRUNNHILDE, TO HER FATHER

I do not want the curious stranger
Staring, the smell of flame brought down

To one awkward moment
When the conflagration dies enough to see

This posture of private waiting:
The place you left, done with me. What work

Keeps you from finishing, finally liable
For what you brought forth. I stayed for the storm;

I thought it between us alone. In your silence,
In the multitude of what you send my way,

The constellations are nothing
Like what I imagined. Your last look

Is what I hold in my hands like a white flower
Open as a bowl for any kind of rain.

REACHING FOR THE LAMP

I imagined much not ours. The business of
What separates us enters the argument
And what you never bring keeps me

In lament and awake. Wax everywhere,
The plates untouched. What I say being
Too loud for the exact shape of how you are

Missing. Like planets across the great meadow
Of sky, one after another until impossible
To tell who leads and who follows. Desire lasting

Only because of refusal. It is not
A good thing to be worshipped. I had to burn
What I could to see. What is left is cloth

Slipped off a pale shoulder, the turned head. All for the sake
Of morning, against which the lamp holds nothing.

THE MISTAKE

did I startle you,
the unexpected light
which was not supposed to be

easy, your face stranger
than in the dark, the distinct
angle a hand wandered,

where I gave myself you,
learning your edge
and where it ended, where my body

was a question I asked,
and instead of answering
you asked another question, which tells me

you do not want me
to know what I know,
the wound made in order

to find a way back. So to fall
for what we finally make
and do with the night

was the mistake: to know nothing
beyond is to have a world
so entire it collapses

around us who are all that is left
in the useless light, that,
and the ruin I keep pulling over us.

THRESHOLD

We got into the room and the room
No longer wanted us. All those dreams
Of arriving suddenly emptied;

The room being all it knows
Of itself, and how we built the room.
What was longing was enough. Inside: the lamp

On the table, cut flowers, done.
Nothing more for us to arrange; you and I standing
With no place else to go. Caught face to face

Until the blink. This, the beginning
Of what the room did. Let the room become
The reason. Let it all be reason, save how

Our eyes move between us, string of
Each end held by the other, taut, quivering.

IN WAITING

Is who might return and when
And is the immaculate night. Is the unravel,
The look down into my hands to see

What they have done, is remnant found each dawn.
Is the graven morning with child
And window, is the phone call never made,

Is the ragged seam gone unnoticed, is the dress worn
Again and again, is the book
Open on the table, is the weight

Of your bracelet on the dresser as daylight finishes
In our old room, is the door not quite closed,
Is the one light from the house in which

You have chosen to live, is the tree
Against clapboards, the bowing and the scrape.

BIRD THAT COMES JUST
BEFORE OUR KISS

A nest held by the cup, by the curve
Of our two throats. Each composed wing; to behold
That arrival, that settling

Into air between us—how she might grow
Tame, how she might eat from our hand! A sound came
In a slight way, but to draw back until

Each feather came into view, the hammer
Of the tiny heart, the underlidded eye,
Became what we did not do. The nearby

Of everything braced as if to ask was it enough
We had come this far. To look up even once
Was to lose the bird and what is made

Out of nowhere and nothing, the open place,
The sudden shape caused by what closes in.

DONE FOR

I did not mean to go so far, to take you
Into my mouth that night on the kitchen floor.
Once the dog tastes blood it is over. To return

Impossible, undone by each tremor,
Struggle, the new small twinge at the back
Of the throat. Limbs ache with what

Cannot stop, places torn open with
Each magnificent rise and fall of the world,
Which is no longer about the plenty

Or the way home, having come down
To only this. She is ruined; she
Who once slept at her master's knee, now the hunted,

Standing in the middle of a field, stunned
By what she holds so delicately in her mouth.

HERE IN THE OPEN

Across your lap like a coat my body;
Cloth to be sewn, stitches finished.
While breath is held the act of anything

Done by each other becomes consequence;
You examine your industry, your hand able
To take on the work of it, large and thorough

In its task. I will keep still, my eye
On your eye, waiting for you to look away.
How to stay along the edge,

Let the ungraceful fasten, perhaps
Become love, a place where it might begin;
How to make of each other a garment, a way

To remain, one holding the other up
Against the blue, the unmistakable trees.

STILL

There, where the light shows. Little sliver
From underneath as I write
And pass this night like many others

Leaning toward what I never thought
I'd get to: it takes most of a love to find
Nothing, not even disappointment,

For in the coming is going, which is how
It becomes dexterity: to remain standing
As the ground moves away, and toward another.

OUT DEEP

We are a boat without love. Love
Works a way through the current,
Headed for us, waving. It is
Unclear to whom she speaks;
It is even possible

Something behind us
Moves her. We came
All this way for the unbroken
Water and such light I can no longer see
Where we are. You must

Guide me: nothing more can be done
If we are to get to shore. In return
I will keep your story,
The one you will tell the others
When we get home.

BREAK ME TO PROVE I AM UNBROKEN

You say you will come
Again; this time I wait through

The extra burning, the vicinity of your
Tongue making a slow way toward beginning and this

Then becomes the argument, the only one
In the collar of moonlight as finally I cause you

To answer your several names. It is all
About return, enough faith to live

On whatever remains. While your hand seeks
The broken glass of what has not

Happened yet, it breaks everything
Along the way. The old vines tighten

Around the untended kingdom while some still sleep
And the long approach

Of no footfall becomes the road I hurry home on
To a place where I learned to leave the body

Not so much in safety but with the best intentions,
And into the smallest space I crawl, a taste of mud,

An edge of light into the room so each morning the world
Can solve itself against the abandoned stones.

HOLY

At the cross of the cross
Is the part that holds. Two roads
Meet; after that is the work of continuing

On. Beyond intersection
Lies departure, which is then to see
What goes on without you, what

Does not go wrong. One tree reconciles
Against another; arm over arm,
A man across a woman in a contract

Of the one thing they know
They do well, which is the beginning
Of how one will soon leave

The other. They cannot turn back
For what they have made in the air
Already discloses agreement, and

Is where many have stopped to rest.

DAMAGE

It is finished. To take myself back
As if trees or even night
Relied on us, shadows we thought

Something. The horses wait over the ridge,
Untethered. Having gone beyond what was
Necessary to survive, we ended up in the middle

Of nowhere, burning
Everything to stay alive. Outside
Is what keeps us by the fire, holding back

The cold. Outside the cage
Is the cage. In which we only see each other—
The dark being all we have left, dark

And the sadness of how it no longer matters
If we stay or go. By heart I know your outline
And the distance which keeps the burning

To be watched over and fed by whatever
Lives between us.

HEAVEN, WHICH IS

I have not handled the ordinary well
And wandered into much time spent
Taking on the unfaithful,

Blunder and flaw. And stayed with it, in the face
Of you who cuts across all landscape,
Who quivers my legs until unable to anymore

Stand and I lie down in an open field,
Wait. Edge and much sky like invitation.
To stay for who comes with message, as in the midst

Of battle, breathless, the coat a little
Torn and in disarray but getting the word out,
Which is how I was finally not for you, which is

What made me irrevocable. No one shall have
What they first believed, and then beyond.
The trail is the story and is

What saves us from going back
To the beginning when we could only see
The other. Through you paradise

Was and paradise
Must fail. One of us might look
Down, or the corner of an eye catch

Movement, a glint, astray. Heaven is only
What it cannot be: either in its zero, its finish
Of balance, or entirely slipped

To one side. Not as place to discover
Anything: the blank page, the white
Noise, the raw of just being there.

III

MESSENGER

So many doves came at dusk I hid. Not
Understanding the music that rose from one tree
I was afraid and waited through the dark

For someone to find me walking down the hall,
Stopping by each window to see if anything
Changed, though I could hear by the noise

They were going on with it, insisting,
The gray tree weeping under the weight
Of all that attention. Wanting to be
The one they sang for, I entered the yard;

Startled, the branches bowed then sprung
Into newfound lightness, each bird
Gone against the sky. They left without telling
Why they sing; they did not know, did not know.

IN CASE OF RAPTURE

As if it were an ordinary day with light
And the car just broke and I cannot figure how
To move it toward where I want to go,

As if I didn't care, as if I could be ruthless
And walk back up that hill, the one with nothing
On it but a fence, a barn and two old cows

Who won't even look up, as if I could walk right in
The big doors and find you, your face no longer dark
As a church but striped with the late angling sun,

Your strong arms swinging bales ever higher, one
On top of another like steps, while below the donkey
And goat announce I've come home, they cannot wait

To eat, as if for one night I could let them cry, our house
Growing cold in the dusk, the cows suddenly lifting
Their heads while I hold you long enough to believe.

HUSBANDRY

My solemn hens. Electric bulb, the door
Locked twice. To keep from hearing the coyote
We dream of the rooster claiming dawn

Even as he flees to the unknown forest.
As I enter all eyes turn golden;
The autumn haunches shift. How quickly they forget

What I have already carried out.
My hand open as if every time I must remember
How they are still here, the sun

Coming fast and against the wind
Each hunkering down. Box by wooden box,
My fingers search for the egg, triumphant

Even in shit, little soul of perfection,
New and impossible, in a crown of straw.

AS SHE GOES

The dream-twitch, her back leg as if running
Through morning woods, only she is dying,
And in the rhythm of each breath unsure

Of the last, her whiskers crushed
Against the green of my old coat, the slow
Deliberate words I had learned to use—

But I cannot move; I wait for any sign
Of forgiveness. Instead, a precise
Tremble of her body as it travels

Through fear, her ear fixed to the ground
As if to some other voice. Instead,
That moment she lifts her head, turns back

And looks direct into my eye, looking
For herself, to see what it is I see.

THE WAY THROUGH

The fence has rotted just enough. A few cows
Push through, tired of patience. Pigs follow,
Then sheep, while the goats who have already

Climbed over, pull down grapevine to browse,
Something to bring along. Unaware of this
Uprising, we continue in the barn, cleaning out

The stalls, changing oil in the tractor. But the animals
Move as if convinced we will follow;
Before them the untouched grass and a simple path

To the far end. Always one more field, and us
Somewhere behind; the long dominion of green and dusk
While each head turns wondering what we bring this time

And with such gravity, as we make our way
Over the pasture, our voices taken up by the wind.

BIRTHDAY

The tree becomes a sign I pass
Of how it has gone on; branches that hold
Up the first stars like waiting candles

Against the coming night. I have learned
To live with less and less
While the child in the backseat sleeps

Believing she is already home.
Out of her hand falls one shoe,
Her mouth stained with whatever kind
Of paradise she has wished for,

And something I had in mind
Darts across the road, a small animal
Moving perfectly between tires
As I look back to see nothing changed.

ICE ON THE POND

Which breaks into chaos, the landscape
To once again manage the seams come undone,
The woken root, rage in the leaves for what

The commonplace did in passing. What is
Underground should not be brought back; too much
Of the dark taken up and the world learns

To depend on what gathers, as if for the first time
And in wonder. So when she whispers,
When she gospels you along the trail, remember

None of it stays exact, even if the moon repeats
In relentless trees, the angle each night
Measured. What becomes a melody carried

Into sleep, or to wake by, is only on the mind
Seeking to have something take hold for once.

THE GUEST

She let him in, who knows what kind of god;
She knew how others hesitated
When he was at their door, the terrible wind

Pushing the latch, and how all this might be
Reckoned at the end. She should have
Known better about the difficult night

Filled with questions, silence as she stirred
What she could into the soup, hardly looking
Up, while a bird at the window watched, while the cow

Called from the barn and the overcoat
He never took off became as dark as
The back of the room, as the hours worked

Along the table. But, after entering,
He did not change her life; her fingers
Like rope that brings up water from the well

Could not let go of each side of her bowl
As she leaned in to hear, to come
Closer to the place where she might ask.

TRIAGE

Nothing else to do
But love while waiting. We hold our hands

To the flames until we no longer know
What we wait for.

THE EMBRACE

when the man cannot love earth
any longer he is also deciding
to leave, when the man believes
we can no longer hold him
up into the light, when the man
is finished with the harm
done to him and those he watches over,

when the man finds I am necessary
face to face, when the man concludes
through me he will get there,
when he puts himself altogether close
with his plan of salvation,
when the man needs to go beyond
my body with his body, to take it

all apart with the slightest turn
of head, finger, a drawing back
of the lip, whatever was true before
now collapsing on itself until
I too have nothing left
except what refuses to burn and the smell
of forgiveness on the breath

THE LAST MINUTE

As you hold the child tight, huddled,
She asks for one more wish and someone pushes

You to the back, yelling you will soon
Be home. Is this moving away or toward—

Even air cannot find where to go,
While you make a way through one last story,

A fumble of buttons, her eyes held to yours
With everything she knows, her voice in

Your voice to drown out the engine
Burning as it was never meant to,

Such acceleration and so much light,
For many are the angels

On their knees, hoping to be first
As the City rises up to greet you

With some on their way to work, some stepping out
To take in the perfect day.

WHERE WE CROSS

How strange to believe in air
Large enough for us all.

No comfort, the thing we live.
The undersong of blood and so much on the mind

Does not know where to go.
If I climb back into what happened,

I might meet you and hold out
What I can toward the eventual,

For we did begin from the one ground,
From where our mothers still watch. What I wish

Is to breathe into your mouth a space
For all this difficult bending, as if

It were beauty, as if it were the only place
Left for those who tried so hard

To hold us apart that we came together.

WHEN ON THE THIRD NIGHT

Turning back, the body became statue
While what tried to reach paradise
Kept landing on the ground beside you

Still in a tremble, the descent of paper
Like birds burning, air no longer
Itself, ash resolving

Everywhere, over trees holding up
Like virtue, like allegory,
Where some try to leave by taking others

With them, where those with something to say
Lie down with those who have nothing,
This place where you could never see

The stars anyway, the avenue, the bars
All shuddering when on the third night
Thunder, and a whole city held its breath.

END OF DAYS

The stranger you saw in the garden that night
Is one who in time finds you. He wants
To give news, the great thing you wait for

And tries each gate with a message, but you
Cannot say you are ready. Also: he is weary
And does not know what to call home so he leans back

Into the dark and you play the music louder,
Certain you heard a noise and you too are tired
Of holding what you want even as you hear it leave

And dare not move. Only at the last
Will you remember where
You saw him. You at the window watching,

Being watched. The delayed light of stars, your arms
Outspread and all the keys pressed down at once.

THEREFORE

To walk back to the first place
As if nothing ever happened
(I save myself however I can)

Here on this beach where I was once certain.
Perhaps you will make me out,
Perhaps this is not the best time to ask,

Perhaps you don't know yet
How you will choose. Perhaps you wander
And look in every face to learn

The words you might use, the ones you have
To give while your finger points
In a special direction. I never thought

You would be like this, you who were so good
At bringing me here, who left
While I got better at staying

(In case you might be watching)
And never giving up, which includes the idea
Even as I am saved, I must also be leaving.

THE OFFERING

Up to the point of no return
Was climbed. Dominion came
Apart when you asked for whatever last

I could give. All along I thought it me
Who wanted to finish this
And that I would know you

By how you finally came. But here at the end,
Borders do not hold, actually
Never existed. I made myself a stranger

To find you. I leaned
Into the wrong sacred, brought
Everything with me. And now the binding

(The difficult act of how much to love)
Loosens itself until only the gift remains
Intact, spared, unwanted.

HE LOOKED DOWN

The shifted stone, vague meadows and mud
Of animals moving, the cross and recross
Of one behind the other so that none

Go missing. Or men on horses or beside horse
Making a way up the mountain
While all over the higher ground damage

Is done, especially in the enterprise
Of return. His plan was to climb until nothing
Was left, to wait for what he did not know

And now he can see each road as it rises,
Gathers and ends in the place where he stands,
Coming to him like spokes of a star,

A wagonwheel, the web of one who looks down
To see what he is not, his outline being the last
Or first to leave: sudden darkness, the mountainside

Cold, each rock holding as much of the day
As possible.

IN LIGHT OF ALL

In light of all that has happened
Which you didn't want to have happen, remember
It was going to happen even as you believed

It could never happen
And as far as knowing what happens next,
Nothing can be done except whatever possible

To make what you want have happen,
To also be present while it is happening,
To be there and to be able to say you were,

And to write it down for someone else to know
They do not know what is happening
So they can say they know what happened

While the light in which all that has happened
Happened in so many ways that finally the light
Became what happened.

AND MORNING STAR

When I looked, when I finally allowed
Looking, there was nothing but my voice,

Noise of my own much too loud for a room
Where the music suddenly stopped. Then a shape

Not unlike myself, only I watched it approach
Like a stranger, one who carried instructions

I had not yet heard but have been ready
To practice at home with those I am familiar

Or at least sleep near; I could never have come
This far without some kind of help, the counselor

Who speaks with us when necessary, who keeps us
Until we no longer remember to leave,

Which then becomes something to love,
Never how you imagined it, wondering what exactly

Took place, how much further you will go.

SOPHIE CABOT BLACK is the author of *The Misunderstanding of Nature*, which won the Poetry Society of America's 1994 Norma Farber First Book Award. She teaches at Columbia University and lives in New York City and Connecticut.

This book was based on a design by Tree Swenson.

It is set in Baskerville type with Goudy titling by Stanton Publication Services,

Inc., and manufactured by Thomson-Shore on acid-free paper.